AF830691

PEARSON

LANGUAGE CENTRAL

ELD Song Book

Grade 4

PEARSON

Glenview, Illinois • Boston, Massachusetts • Chandler, Arizona • Upper Saddle River, New Jersey

Acknowledgments

Cover: Tim Jessell

Unit 1 Week 1 Dan Santat; Week 2 Suwin Chan; Week 3 Donald Wu; Week 4 Paule Trudel; Week 5 Erica Pelton Vilnave

Unit 2 Week 1 Matt Luxich; Week 2 Robert Dress; Week 3 Eldon Doty; Week 4 Erin Eitter Kono; Week 5 Damien Ward

Unit 3 Week 1 Sarah Dillard; Week 2 Suwin Chan; Week 3 Erica Pelton Vilnave; Week 4 Dan Santat; Week 5 Matt Luxich

Unit 4 Week 1 Sue Williams; Week 2 Alan Flinn; Week 3 Donald Wu; Week 4 Johanna Van der Sterre; Week 5 Paule Trudel

Unit 5 Week 1 Jessica Secheret; Week 2 Robert Dress; Week 3 Dan Santat; Week 4 Matt Luxich; Week 5 Damien Ward

Unit 6 Week 1 Barroux; Week 2 Erica Pelton Vilnave; Week 3 Orlando Ramirez; Week 4 Suwin Chan; Week 5 Gabriel Carranza

ISBN-13: 978-0-328-65823-7
ISBN-10: 0-328-65823-5

3 4 5 6 7 8 9 10 V0ZN 13

PEARSON LANGUAGE CENTRAL

Table of Contents

All Kinds of People

Tune: "Down by the Station"

All kinds of people
Often get together,
Folks from different places
Share things as one.
Each person comes from
A different kind of **culture,**
But sharing together
Can be a lot of fun!

Music is a thing that
People share together.

Crowds **appreciate** it,
Though they are **diverse.**
Music from a **banjo**
Brings folks together,
Enjoyed by many people
Across the universe!

Opportunities

Tune: "Bingo"

Great-Grandpa was an **immigrant.**
He came for higher **wages.**
Possibilities
Waited overseas.
Opportunities
Are found in brand new places!

Great-Grandpa found a place to live,
And then he found **employment**
At the **cannery,**
In this land that's free!
Opportunities
Are found in brand new places!

Great-Grandpa's memory lives on
In stories that we cherish.
We're his legacies:
Grandpa, Mom, and me!
Opportunities
Are found in brand new places!

Travel the U.S.A.

Tune: "Daisy, Daisy, Give Me Your Answer, Do"

Travel, travel,
Travel the U.S.A.
Countless places
We visit along the way.
The **towering cliffs** and mountains,
The rivers, lakes, and fountains,
And we can see our history
As we visit the sights each day!

Travel, travel,
Travel the U.S.A.

On the **highway,**
Driving so far, I'll say!
The **plains** seem to go for miles,
The whole trip brings me smiles.
I've **longed** to see our great country,
Now I've seen it, and here I'll stay!

The Southwest

Tune: "My Darling Clementine"

I have traveled across the country,
And I think one part is best.
In the West and in the South,
It's the land called the Southwest.

Oh, the **landscape** is amazing,
See an eagle in its nest.
See a mountain, see a **riverbed**
In the land called the Southwest.

In the **desert,** there's a rabbit,
See a **tortoise** stop and rest,
See a **cactus** standing proudly
In the land called the Southwest.

If you travel across the country,
You may think one part is best.
In the West and in the South,
It's the land called the Southwest.

Question of the Week: How does Yosemite reflect the unique qualities of the West?

5
The West
Grade 4, Unit 1, Week 5
ELD

Out West in Yosemite

Tune: "This Old Man"

CHORUS:
There's a park you should see,
It is called Yosemite.
It is so **impressive,** as pretty as can be,
Out West in Yosemite!

Wilderness very wide,
Where many creatures hunt and hide.
It's a **habitat** where animals run free,
Out West in Yosemite!

Hear the roar of a **waterfall,**
See a **sequoia** standing tall.
In a **meadow,** pretty flowers you will see,
Out West in Yosemite!

CHORUS

People with Talent

Tune: "The Yellow Rose of Texas"

All people have a **talent,**
Something that they do well,
And if you watch them closely,
Their talent you can tell.
When someone has a talent,
Then here's what you should do:
Appreciate what they can do,
It may rub off on you!

All **athletes** have a talent,
They're very good at play,
When they **compete** with others,
They try hard all the way!

There's talent in all athletes
And other people, too.
Appreciate what they can do,
It may rub off on you!

Working Together

Tune: "On Top of Old Smoky"

By working together,
By working as one,
A job goes much faster,
And quickly it's done.

To round up wild horses
May not be much fun,
But a roundup goes faster
When a team works as one.

In the **distance,** a cow **herd**
Has gone off the track.

But a good team of **ranch** hands
Can bring them right back.

By working together,
You feel so **relieved.**
By working together,
See what you **achieve!**

Question of the Week What obstacles stand in the way of teamwork?

Teamwork

Tune: "The Eensy Weensy Spider"

When you practice **teamwork,**
You work as a team.
Working together
Is harder than it seems.
A group must agree
How to get the job done.
If an **argument** breaks out,
Then teamwork isn't fun.

With a lot of teamwork,
You will be amazed.
But when you argue,
An **obstacle** is **raised.**

It's always better
To try to get along.
A group that uses teamwork
Will always be strong!

Question of the Week How do animals help with our work?

9 Animals Grade 4, Unit 2, Week 4 ELD

Animals Help

Tune: "I've Been Working on the Railroad"

Animals, animals,
How they help out!
Horses on ranches
Take people about.
Horse **transportation**
Is helpful, it's true.
Thank the animal helpers
For the job they do!

Animals, animals,
Dogs are so kind,
Helping police out
And walking with the **blind.**

Special dog **training**
Is helpful, it's true.
Thank the animal helpers
For the job they do!

The President

Tune: "If You're Happy and You Know It"

If you're President, you're leader of the land,
If you're President, you're leader of the land,
Yes, if you're the President,
Then you head our **government,**
If you're President, you're leader of the land!

If you're President, **decisions** must be made,
If you're President, decisions must be made,
You must act **seriously,**
Take **responsibility,**
If you're President, decisions must be made.

If you're President, the **White House** is your home,
If you're President, the White House is your home,
You meet people, quite a few,
Often you give **speeches,** too,
If you're President, the White House is your home.

Autumn

Tune: "Camptown Races"

Of all **seasons**, which is best?
Autumn, autumn!
So much nicer than the rest,
Yes, the autumn's here!

Look outside and see the **frost**,
Autumn, autumn!
Watch the leaves get blown and tossed,
Yes, the autumn's here!

CHORUS:
See the autumn leaves
Falling to the ground!

Red and yellow, brown and gold,
Autumn is around!

Leaves pile up, they never stop,
Autumn, autumn!
Temperature begins to drop,
Yes, the autumn's here!

I am **fascinated** by
Autumn, autumn!
How I love the autumn sky,
Yes, the autumn's here!

CHORUS

Animals Migrate

Tune: "Did You Ever See a Lassie?"

CHORUS:

Do you know the many creatures
That **migrate,** that migrate?
Do you know the many creatures
That move when it's cold?

Some butterflies find spaces
In **tropical** places.
Do you know the many creatures
That move when it's cold?

CHORUS

Birds fly in **formation,**
A **pattern,** a pattern.
Birds fly in formation
To move where it's warm.

The clouds are above them,
The earth helps to **guide** them.
Birds fly in formation
To move where it's warm.

Tales of Day and Night

Tune: "Little Brown Jug"

CHORUS:
Long ago, folks would say,
"What brings on the night and day?"
It was a **mystery,**
Such a curiosity!

People shared great **delights**
Telling tales of days and nights.
Every **myth** sounded right;
They explained the dark and light.

CHORUS

All the myths were such fun,
Some explained the **brilliant** sun.
Some told why the moon **gleams;**
Every myth made sense, it seems!

CHORUS

Watch Out for a Storm

Tune: "Bingo"

If someone **forecasts** storms ahead,
You really must be careful!

CHORUS:
Watch out for a storm!
Watch out for a storm!
Watch out for a storm!
You really must be careful!

A **funnel** on the radar screen
Means strong winds are coming!

CHORUS

A **violent** storm is very bad,
It causes great **destruction.**

CHORUS

Unstable winds will blow so hard
That everything goes flying!

CHORUS

Weather Changes

Tune: "Home on the Range"

It may seem quite strange
How the weather can change,
How a day can turn so hot or cold.
But we can explain
Hot and cold, snow and rain,
It's a **challenge,** but it can be told.

CHORUS:
Change, change through the year,
Weather changes are felt far and near.
Though weather is **untamed,**
And though no one's to blame,
There will be changes, that much is clear.

A **cowboy** out West
May be put to the test
When rain's pouring down from the sky.
A sailor at sea
May be scared as can be
When the **sea level** rises too high.

CHORUS

Question of the Week: Can you always believe what you see?

16
Perception
Grade 4, Unit 4, Week 1
ELD

Don't Believe It!

Tune: "Twinkle, Twinkle, Little Star"

When you watch what people do,
Do you think it's always true?
A good **magician** plays a trick,
Performing it so very quick.
When you watch what people do,
Don't believe it's always true!

When a magician does an act,
A good **assistant** may **distract.**
The **audience** just sees her **escape,**
But can't see what's behind the cape.
How amazing it looks to you,
But the **illusion** isn't true!

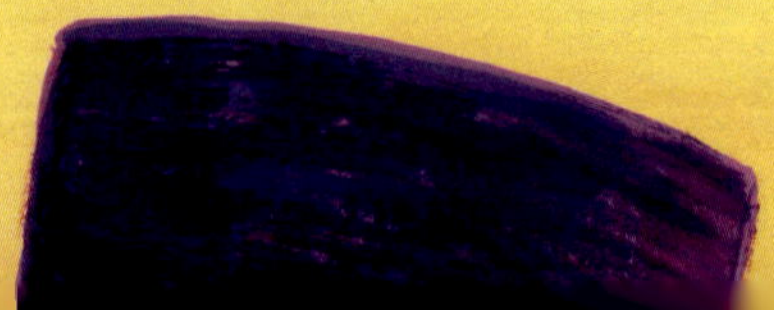

How Animals Behave

Tune: "The Eensy Weensy Spider"

Animals **behave**
In the most amazing ways.
They often follow patterns
When at work or play.
Whether they're **aquatic**
Or living on land,
Animals behave in ways
We try to understand.

Deep in the ocean,
Whales **communicate.**
They sing special songs
To try to find their **mates.**

A yearly **migration**
Is something else they do,
And people are **enchanted**
By how they act, it's true!

It's a Secret

Tune: "Hush, Little Baby, Don't Say a Word"

Hush, my friend, please don't say a word.
I've got a secret that no one's heard.

There is a secret **route** I know,
With a secret **station** where we can go.

If you're **enslaved**, you'll soon be free.
Don't tell anyone, just come with me.

I will lead you along the way,
We'll share **messages** every day.

The trip's **exhausting** and it's slow,
But you'll be **protected** wherever you go.

So hush, my friend, just come with me.
Keep it a secret, and soon you'll be free!

Question of the Week How can knowing another language create understanding?

19

Communication
Grade 4, Unit 4, Week 4

ELD

Hieroglyphics

Tune: "Alouette"

CHORUS:

Hieroglyphics,
What are hieroglyphics?
Hieroglyphics,
An **ancient** way to write.

See the **symbols** on that wall?
Scholars understand them all.
On that wall, see them all,
Oh!

CHORUS

Writings from an early date,
We are able to **translate.**
Early date, we translate,
Oh!

CHORUS

Language from so long ago
Tells us facts we want to know.
Long ago, facts we know,
Oh!

CHORUS

Look for Details

Tune: "My Bonnie Lies Over the Ocean"

If you are a **detective**
Who wants to solve a **crime,**
Then you must look for **details,**
One detail at a time.

CHORUS:
Each detail is important,
Each detail has its place, its place.
By studying the details,
You can solve the case!

A **diamond** has been stolen,
You're **stumped,** what do you do?

You look for any **fingerprints,**
Yes, they're a helpful clue!

Hooray! You found the jewelry.
Hooray! You solved the crime.
You won by finding details,
One detail at a time!

CHORUS

Ready for an Emergency

Tune: "The Farmer in the Dell"

Be ready as can be
For an **emergency.**
Be ready with the things you'll need
In an emergency.

All pilots flying high
Are ready in the sky.
Each **pilot** has a parachute
For an emergency.

All firefighters know
What to bring when they go.

A ladder helps them **rescue** folks
In an emergency.

The driver on a bus
Knows roads are **dangerous.**
A first-aid kit is always there
For an emergency.

On an Expedition

Tune: "Oh, Susanna"

Going on an **expedition**
Is exciting as can be!
For as you go, you never know
What ancient things you'll see.

You may find ancient **ruins**
Of a **palace** in the sand.
Its **glorious** past will come alive
As you explore the land.

CHORUS:
Expedition!
Travel far and wide.

Things once enjoyed but now **destroyed**
Are hidden by your side!

Expedition!
It can be a blast!
For nothing is **impossible**
When you dig up the past!

Be a Hero

Tune: "I'm a Little Teapot"

You can be a **hero,**
Yes, you can!
All that it takes
Is a simple plan.
If someone is in need,
Then help them out.
You're a hero,
There's no doubt!

You will be a hero,
Yes, you'll be,
When you help others
Confidently.

Always act brave,
Not **nervously,**
And a hero
You will be!

Unknown Places

Tune: "My Bonnie Lies Over the Ocean"

Explorers take plenty of chances,
And **scientists** take chances, too.
They travel to far, **unknown** places
To study a place that is new.

CHORUS:
Danger, danger,
It's dangerous in the unknown, unknown!
Danger, danger,
It's dangerous in the unknown.

Explorers are faced with excitement,
But often it comes with a price.
They work with such great **anticipation,**
A calm life they must **sacrifice.**

CHORUS

A Walk on the Moon

Tune: "The Wheels on the Bus"

A walk on the moon is **challenging**,
Challenging, challenging.
A walk on the moon is challenging,
Up, oh so high!

Astronauts put **spacesuits** on,
Spacesuits on, spacesuits on.
Astronauts put spacesuits on,
Up, oh so high!

An astronaut walks with lots of care,
Lots of care, lots of care.

An astronaut walks with lots of care,
Up, oh so high!

They're **weightless** for there's no **gravity**,
Gravity, gravity.
They're weightless for there's no gravity,
Up, oh so high!

Words, Words

Tune: "Skip to My Lou"

CHORUS:

Words, words, we all use words,
Words, words, we all use words,
Words, words, we all use words,
Words have a great **importance!**

All ideas we wish to state
Need words to communicate.
The power of words is truly great,
Words have a great importance!

CHORUS

Numerous words we have to use,
Numerous words we have to choose,
With the right words, you can't lose!
Words have a great importance!

CHORUS

Many words aloud are said,
Other words are quietly read,
Some use **sign language** instead,
Words have a great importance!

CHORUS

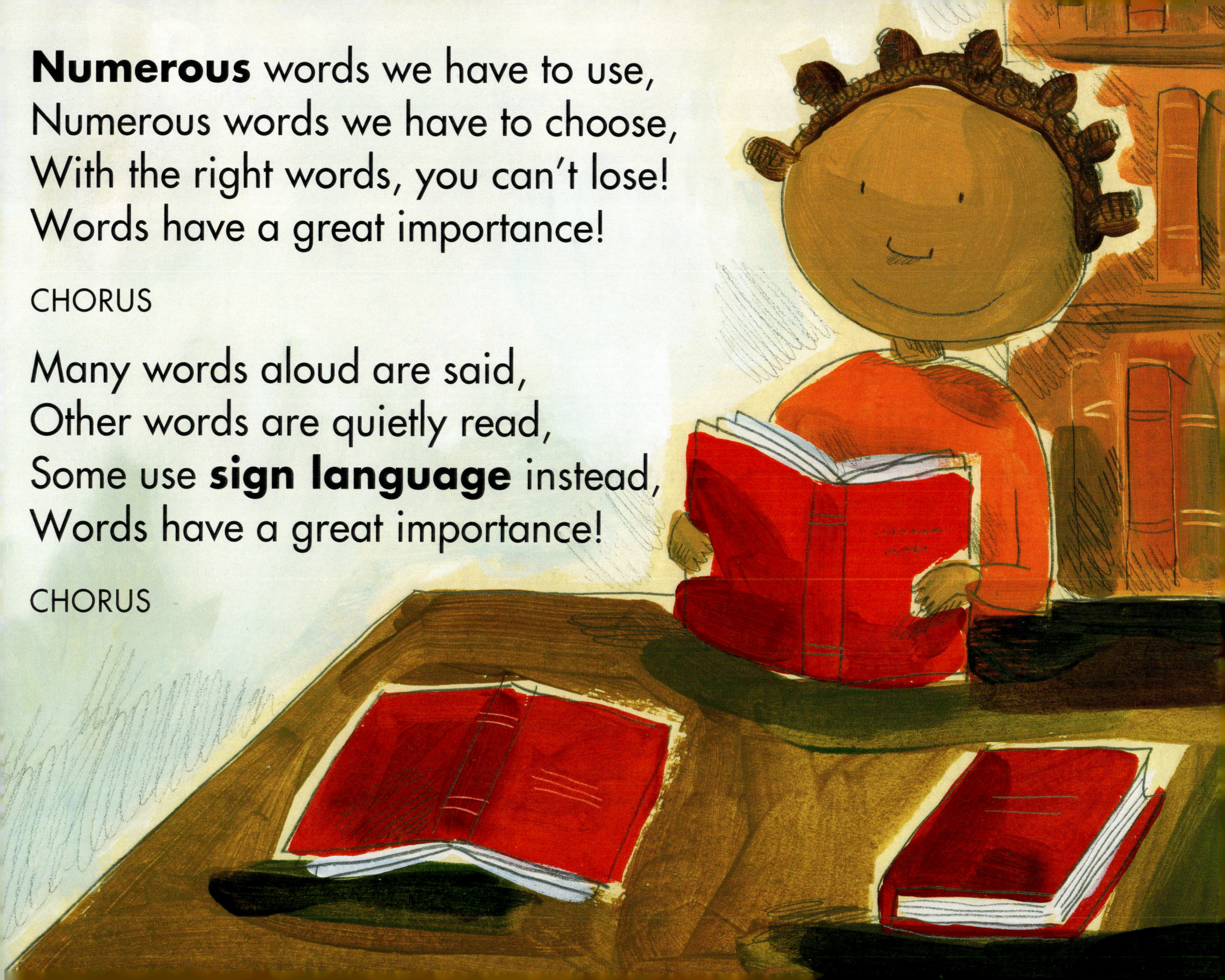

Be the Best!

Tune: "Little Brown Jug"

CHORUS:
Be the best you can be,
Use all your **ability!**
Do your best, and when you're done,
You will be a **champion!**

Always try, never stop,
You will wind up at the top!
Great **endurance** is the key,
Use all your ability!

CHORUS

Don't give up, count to ten,
If **rejected,** start again!
Take a chance, try to be bold,
Win the **medal,** win the gold!

CHORUS

Question of the Week How can one person's view of the world affect others?

28
Coming to a New Culture
Grade 4, Unit 6, Week 3
ELD

A New World

Tune: "Sailing, Sailing, Over the Bounding Main"

Coming, coming,
Coming to a new land,
It may seem so **unusual,**
There's much to understand!
Meeting, meeting,
Meeting new people there.
Their different ways are strange and **quaint,**
But you've got a lot to share!

Learning, learning,
Learning in your new home,
Where nothing may seem **realistic**
When at first you roam!

Sharing, sharing,
Sharing the things you do.
You'll learn a lot from your new friends,
And they'll learn a lot from you!

Reach Your Goal

Tune: "Row, Row, Row Your Boat"

CHORUS:
Work, work very hard,
Climb right up the pole!
Keep on going, never stop
Until you reach your goal!

When you're on the **field,**
Practice and **improve.**
Do it once, then once again,
Hurry! Quickly! Move!

If you slip and fall,
Keep a happy mood.

Get right up and start again,
Show some **fortitude!**

CHORUS

Astronauts Are Heroes

Tune: "Oh Susanna"

Our astronauts are heroes,
They're heroes we admire.
They've done so many great things,
They make us feel **inspired!**

They travel high in **orbit,**
They travel very far.
And all of us look up to them,
For each one is a star!

So busy in the **capsule,**
So busy in the **hatch,**

Each astronaut's **achievement**
Is one we'd like to match!

Our astronauts are heroes,
They're heroes we admire.
They've done so many great things,
They make us feel inspired!